FLORENCE
THE CITY AT A GLANCE

GW01044292

Ponte Vecchio
Dating back to 1345, this bridge
gamut of Florentine life, from g
buskers and peddlers to the tou

Vasari Corridor
A secret passageway connecting the Palazzo
Vecchio with Palazzo Pitti, now hung with self-
portraits by Titian and others (T 055 265 4321).

Instituto e Museo di Storia della Scienza
A synapse-crackling collection of scientific
objects once owned by the Medici family,
including Galileo's compass and telescope.
Piazza dei Giudici 1, T 055 265 311

Galleria degli Uffizi
Vasari's 1581 porticoes and loggia house one
of the world's most visited art collections.
Piazzale degli Uffizi 6, T 055 294 883

Palazzo Vecchio
Once the seat of the Italian parliament, this
clumsy palace is redeemed by Il Cronaca's
elegant Salone dei Cinquecento.
See p012

Basilica di San Lorenzo
The city's first cathedral boasts bronze pulpits
by Donatello and flags its most famous market.
Piazza di San Lorenzo 9, T 055 216 634

Museo del Bargello
Unmissable and crowd-free Renaissance
sculpture and weaponry, such as Donatello's
bronze *David* and Michelangelo's *Bacchus*.
See p034

Duomo
The basilica still dominates the city skyline
with its colossal Brunelleschi-designed dome.
See p010

INTRODUCTION
THE CHANGING FACE OF THE URBAN SCENE

The Renaissance has finally eaten itself. Some nine million tourists (that's 25 to every local) flood this city's palazzi, churches, galleries and museums each year, vying for a glimpse of Giotto, Donatello or Michelangelo genius. The artistic hubris of the city's ruling classes – the Guelphs and Ghibellines in the 13th and 14th centuries, then the Medicis for more than 300 years – has a lot to answer for.

Yet, despite the crowds, the city remains one of the most edifying and alluring in Italy. Its surfeit of pristine cultural riches means that it's possible to find crowd-free wonders just by walking a few extra yards from the centre. And it's not all about ancient marvels. Modern architects such as Mario Botta and the late Giovanni Michelucci have left their mark, while Michele Bönan has spent the past decade creating some of Europe's slickest hotels and bars.

The trick is to treat Florence as two cities separated by the river. The 'rive gauche' district south of the Arno has just come into its own, via high-quality *trattorie*, late-night bars, characterful shops and, most tellingly, Florentines arriving en masse. Spend most of your time here, with just the occasional dip into the more frantic north. And, if you can, visit the city in the quieter months between October and March as the local bowl topography makes for airless, sweltering summers. Most importantly, hire a bike, which will give you the power to zip along to Florence's further-flung treasures, scattering the tourist hordes in your wake like pigeons.

ESSENTIAL INFO
FACTS, FIGURES AND USEFUL ADDRESSES

TOURIST OFFICE
Via Manzoni 16
T 055 23 320
firenzeturismo.it

TRANSPORT
Car hire
Avis
T 055 213 629
Hertz
T 055 307 370
Taxis
So.co.ta
T 055 42 42

EMERGENCY SERVICES
Ambulance
T 118
Fire
T 115
Police
T 113
24-hour pharmacy
Farmacia Comunale 13
Stazione Santa Maria Novella
T 055 216 761

CONSULATES
British Consulate
Lungarno Corsini 2
T 055 284 133
ukinitaly.fco.gov.uk
US Consulate
Lungarno Vespucci 38
T 055 266 951
florence.usconsulate.gov

MONEY
American Express
Via de'Monari 2c, Bologna
T 051 239 950
travel.americanexpress.com

POSTAL SERVICES
Post Office
Via Pellicceria 3
T 055 273 6481
poste.it
Shipping
UPS
T 800 877 877
ups.com

BOOKS
Florence: The City and Its Architecture
by Richard Goy (Phaidon Press)
The Divine Comedy by Dante Alighieri
(Oxford World's Classics)
**The Italian Renaissance: Culture
and Society in Italy** by Peter Burke
(Polity Press)
The Italians by Luigi Barzini (Penguin)

WEBSITES
Art
www.firenzemusei.it
Arts/Culture
firenze2009.it
Newspapers
www.theflorentine.net
lanazione.ilsole24ore.com/firenze
corrierefiorentino.corriere.it

COST OF LIVING
**Taxi from Vespucci Airport to
city centre**
£21
Cappuccino
£1.10
Packet of cigarettes
£4.45
Daily newspaper
£0.92
Bottle of champagne
£65

FLORENCE
Area
102 sq km
Population
366,500
Currency: euro
€1 = £0.93 = $1.29
Telephone codes
Italy: 39
Florence: 055
Time
GMT +1

AVERAGE TEMPERATURE / °C

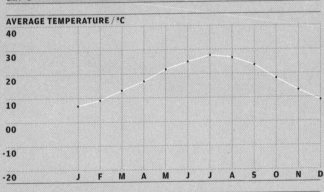

| | J | F | M | A | M | J | J | A | S | O | N | D |

AVERAGE RAINFALL / MM

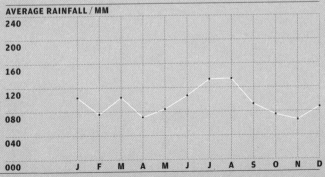

| | J | F | M | A | M | J | J | A | S | O | N | D |

NEIGHBOURHOODS

THE AREAS YOU NEED TO KNOW AND WHY

To help you navigate the city, we've chosen the most interesting districts (see below and the map inside the back cover) and colour-coded our featured venues, according to their location; those venues that are outside these areas are not coloured.

SANTA MARIA NOVELLA

Giovanni Michelucci's rationalist railway station and San Lorenzo market provide workaday antidotes to this area's key Renaissance attractions, which include the frescoes at the Cappella dei Magi (Via Cavour 3, T 055 276 0340) and baroque Chiesa di Ognissanti (Via Borgo Ognissanti 42). The area is also an accommodation hub, with the revamped Piazza Santa Maria Novella home to upmarket hotels such as JK Place (see p028).

SAN MARCO

The Orto Botanico (Via Pier Antonio Micheli 3, T 055 275 7402), Four Seasons' Giardino della Gherardesca (see p017) and Giardino di Palazzo Capponi (Via Gino Capponni 26, T 329 706 6422) make up the northern city's green lung. The obvious art draw is the Galleria dell'Accademia (Via Ricasoli 60, T 055 238 8609), but the 1588 Museo dell'Opificio delle Pietre (Via degli Alfani 78, T 055 294 111) is also worth a visit.

CAMPO DI MARTE

Florence's sporting hot zone offers top-notch footie clashes at the Stadio Artemio Franchi (see p090), the home ground of ACF Fiorentina, and five-a-side knockabouts and egalitarian exercise classes at Atletica Firenze Marathon (see p094). Pushing south, you will reach one of Florence's modern architectural highlights, the avant-garde Sacro Cuore (see p013), designed by the Italian architect Lando Bartoli.

OLTRARNO

Locals flee south of the river to avoid the stampedes in Disneyland Florence. Now a fully fledged artisanal enclave, its bars are the place for some serious intellectual posturing, while the 'rive gauche' streets of Santo Spirito and San Frediano offer great shopping. Cultural stops include Palazzo Pitti (see p009), behind which are the Boboli gardens, and Brancacci's chapel in the Chiesa Santa Maria del Carmine (Piazza del Carmine, T 055 238 2195).

SANTA CROCE

This is where the natives have mustered a feisty rearguard action. Reasons to visit include the city's most authentic food market on Piazza Lorenzo Ghiberti and Fabio Picchi's Cibrèo (see p046). Even the Renaissance attractions are relatively stress-free, including the rambling Basilica di Santa Croce (see p065) and the Sinagoga and Museo di Arte e Storia Ebraica (Via Luigi Carlo Farini 4, T 055 245 252).

SAN GIOVANNI

Shoals of somnambulant tourists swim across the heart of the *centro storico*, while the savvy head to the upscale stores on Via de' Tornabuoni, which include Olfattorio (see p073). The Duomo (see p010) is the unmissable star, though the queues for the Galleria degli Uffizi (Piazzale degli Uffizi 6, T 055 294 883) wrap around its central *piazzale*. The Ponte Vecchio is your escape route south to Oltrarno.

LANDMARKS

THE SHAPE OF THE CITY SKYLINE

Florence's skyline has changed little in the past 600 years. The Duomo (overleaf), crowned by Brunelleschi's 15th-century dome, is still the highest structure in the city, while palazzi such as the Medici's dazzling inaugural seat, Palazzo Medici Riccardi (Via Camillio Cavour 1, T 055 276 0340), continue to steal the limelight. Admittedly, the Nuovo Palazzo di Giustizia (see p014) to the north-west is unashamedly new, but for city-centre cutting edge the Fascist-era efforts in the Stazione Santa Maria Novella (Piazza della Stazione, T 055 235 6120) vein will have to suffice.

If you want to get the measure of Florence, stroll up to Piazza Michelangelo. Here you'll see the Arno scythe through the world's finest Renaissance city. On the north side of the river, the medieval crush can be overwhelming: Palazzo del Bargello (see p034) is jammed in next to the Galleria degli Uffizi (Piazzale degli Uffizi 6, T 055 294 883), while ecclesiastical heavyweights like Basilica di Santa Croce (see p065) to the east or Basilica di San Lorenzo (Piazza San Lorenzo 9, T 055 216 634) to the north – the site of the city's first cathedral – dwarf everything around them. By contrast, the south bank has room to breathe. Beyond Palazzo Pitti (Piazza Pitti 1, T 055 294 8611) are Niccolò Tribolo's Boboli Gardens and Via di San Leonardo, a sliver of a lane dotted with villas, one of which was once inhabited by Tchaikovsky.
For full addresses, see Resources.

Duomo

The real point of Florence's marble-clad cathedral is its sheer, fear-of-God bulk, which seems to stretch Piazza del Duomo at the seams. From here, admire Arnolfo di Cambio's 13th-century structure, the engineering genius of the double-shelled cupola, and Emilio De Fabris's 1887 neo-Gothic façade. *Piazza del Duomo 17, T 055 230 2885, duomofirenze.it*

Palazzo Vecchio

With its 94m-high belltower, this fortified palazzo, completed in 1299, is a spiky reminder of the city's brief stint as Italy's capital; the parliament was based here between 1865 and 1870. Originally designed by Arnolfo di Cambio to house the city's priors, it was tinkered with by Michelozzo, Vasari and Buontalenti over the next 300 years, resulting in a lop-sided affair dominating Piazza della Signoria.

These days, it's a handy reference point for tourists tramping from the Duomo (see p010) to the Uffizi, but to look no further than the replica of Michelangelo's *David* out front would be a mistake. Inside lies the glittering Salone dei Cinquecento, and Francesco I's studio, with secret cabinets used to guard his scientific breakthroughs. *Piazza della Signoria, T 055 276 8325, www.comune.fi.it*

Sacro Cuore

It's hard not to be moved by Lando Bartoli's 1961 church, on the east side of town towards the Stadio Artemio Franchi (see p090). The building's charm lies in the radical interpretation of classic features: a strutted belltower, built with the help of the architect and structural engineer Pierluigi Nervi, is fused onto the main body by eight concrete pillars; windows gleam with abstract stained glass by Felice Quentin, and Giovanni Haynal's *The Way of the Cross* mosaic runs along the entire length of the church. The design clincher has to be the confession boxes – Mario Botta-style brick affairs that look more like the showers in a design hotel. Tradition does get a look in: the façade is green-and-white Prato marble and Angelo Biancini's doors depict biblical scenes.

Via Capo di Mondo 60, T 055 670 148

Nuovo Palazzo di Giustizia

A crash-landed spaceship? A brick-and-glass fantasy plucked from an Italo Calvino fable? This collapsed deck of cards is actually the city's new law courts and university campus, which form the centrepieces of a 32-hectare, 2008-2009 scheme on the site of the old Fiat plant in Novoli, to the north-west of the city centre. Considering most modern structures in Florence are strangled at birth, it's remarkable that the late Leonardo Ricci's behemoth has risen from the dust at all: a brownstone jumble of jarring angles, flanked by blocks of shops, offices and flats. At 64m, it's the second tallest structure in town, sensibly doffing its cap to the 115m Duomo (see p010).
Viale Alessandro Guidoni

HOTELS
WHERE TO STAY AND WHICH ROOMS TO BOOK

A decade ago, lumbering five-star beasts roamed central Florence, sucking visitors into their brocade-and-chandelier-draped innards. Enter an era of cheap flights, swooping in hip weekenders, and the city's hotels had to rustle up some smart alternatives, fast.

The Ferragamo-owned Lungarno group and architect/designer Michele Bönan are the prime movers in the anti-chintz backlash. The luxury brand launched Hotel Lungarno (Borgo San Jacopo 14, T 055 27 261) in 1997, following this with the Gallery Hotel Art (see p020) and Continentale Contemporary Pleasing Hotel (Vicolo dell'Oro 6r, T 055 27 262) in 2003. JK Place (see p028), another Bönan triumph, has also thwarted the old guard. Elsewhere, Riva Lofts (see p021) takes the small-is-beautiful formula even further, offering apartment stays for design-hungry jetsetters. The colourful Stanze di Santa Croce (Via delle Pinzochere 6, T 347 259 3010) and the rustic Le Tre Stanze (Via dell'Oriuolo 43, T 329 212 8756), run by sculptor Patrick-John Steiner, are also recommended.

The behemoths are still here but they have evolved. Olga Polizzi's makeover has done wonders for the Savoy (Piazza della Repubblica 7, T 055 27 351), and the revamped Westin Excelsior (Piazza Ognissanti 3, T 055 27 151) is now a slick, if a little sterile, business-friendly option. Hearteningly, perhaps, the Helvetia & Bristol (Via dei Pescioni 2, T 055 26 651) shows no sign of change. *For full addresses, see Resources.*

Four Seasons Hotel

If your dream abode is a pope's bedroom with all mod cons, stay at this extravagant five-star 15 minutes' walk north-east of the Duomo (see p010). Architects RDM and interior designer Pierre Yves Rochon took this erstwhile palace and convent (the previous owners included Pope Leo XI) and remade it in 2008 as a vision of rococo splendour: 116 rooms full of original frescoes and bas-reliefs, set amid 11 acres of lush gardens, which include an outdoor pool. The aesthetic peaks in the Royal Suite (above and overleaf), while Room 122 offers succour in the form of oriental-style wallpaper. If you can't stay here, at least dine at Vito Mollica's first-class Il Palagio and admire Jan van der Straet's frescoes in the chapel-turned-library. *Borgo Pinti 99, T 055 26 261, fourseasons.com/florence*

Gallery, Royal Suite, Four Seasons Hotel

Gallery Hotel Art

This Lungarno establishment, launched in 2000, helped spearhead the art-hotel movement in Italy. These days, it is somewhat overshadowed by its sibling, the Continentale Contemporary Pleasing Hotel (T 055 27 262), just over the road, but Michele Bönan's interiors and its revamped bar still manage to draw a cool crowd. The library is a highlight: a laid-back lounge with a huge Japanese-style wenge bookcase blocking out the back wall. The oriental theme continues in the 74 rooms, via leather headboards, local stone and wood floors. The Penthouse San Miniato (above) is our pick, all creamy tones and super views across the city. *Vicolo dell'Oro 5, T 055 27 263, lungarnohotels.com*

Riva Lofts

Built out of an artisan workshop on the south bank of the Arno, Claudio Nardi's eight suites, opened in 2006, are beacons of minimalism amid a sea of rococo clichés. The feel is stylish Tuscan farmhouse meets slick city dwelling. The sitting room is a vaulted space with an open fire, a home cinema and wi-fi, and a mix of vintage and modern furniture, and the suites are done out with soft grey hues, resin floors and clever features such as concealed hobs and sinks. Studio Seven opens onto the garden, with its strip of a pool, while one of the loft studios (above) has a four-poster bed and a private terrace. It's a 15-minute bike ride into town (the perfect distance to slough off the freneticism of the city) and wheels are provided.
Via Baccio Bandinelli 98,
T 055 713 0272, rivahotel.it

Villa La Vedetta

Its prime hillside location, just south of the river, steps from Piazzale Michelangelo, is just one reason to stay at this elegant neo-Renaissance villa. Formerly a private residence, it was restored in 2003 by architect Piera Tempesti Benelli to house a tranquil luxury retreat. Inside, Venetian mosaic floors and salvaged 19th-century fireplaces blend seamlessly with Baccarat chandeliers and contemporary furniture, as in the lobby (above). The 18 rooms each have bathrooms with marble jacuzzis. We were especially impressed by the Bellavista Suite, with its views of Brunelleschi's cupola (see p010), and the rooms in the more private Villa Romantica, which is set apart from the main building. The in-house Onice lounge/restaurant is top-notch. Fresh produce is supplied by La Vedetta's own vegetable garden.
Viale Michelangelo 78, T 055 681 631, www.villalavedettahotel.com

UNA Hotel Vittoria
Swirling stained glass and seats that rear and arch like giant strips of orange peel are architect Fabio Novembre's artful foils to the gubbins of business-friendly mod cons in this 83-room hotel, open since 2003. The Executive Rooms (pictured) boast freestanding baths and a sleek scheme of black and green. Plasma TVs and wi-fi are standard in all.
Via Pisana 59, T 055 22 771, unahotels.it

Relais Santa Croce

This conversion of the 18th-century Ciofi-Jacometti Palace ticks every box: central location, genuine five-star opulence and vast baths. It was reborn as a hotel after a 2004 renovation by Elio Baccianti and Marco Garganti. Trad successfully accommodates modern, with restored frescoes sitting alongside art deco-style lacquer tables by Patrizia Garganti's Baga brand and Reza Yah Yaei's abstract paintings. The grandiose lounge, open fires and upmarket restaurant, Guelfi e Ghibelline, give the impression of a more substantial hotel, but there are just 24 rooms, including 13 suites. Try to reserve the 90 sq m Dei Pepi (above) or 170 sq m Da Verrazzano, offered with a personal butler service if you wish. *Via Ghibellina 87, T 055 234 2230, relaisantacroce.com*

Palazzo Tornabuoni

You might not fancy the full-time upkeep of a 15th-century palazzo, but a part-time piece of this sort of action is on offer at Palazzo Tornabuoni, a 'private residence club' managed by the Four Seasons group, due for completion at the end of 2009. In this palace once owned by Alessandro de' Medici (later Pope Leo XI), architects and restorers have carved out 36 apartments, including the Michelozzo Suite (above), installing new fittings, such as custom-designed Boffi kitchens, and bringing a fresh lustre to the statuary, mosaics and frescoes. Residents will have access to a fitness room, wine bar and cellar, and visits can be arranged to private art collections. A chauffeur-driven Maserati Quattroporte will be at guests' disposal.

Via Tornabuoni 16, T 055 268 966
palazzotornabuoni.com

JK Place

More millionaire's retreat than boutique hotel, the 20-room JK Place is the most spirited accommodation in town. Opened in 2003, on the edge of the Piazza Santa Maria Novella, its canvas is classical – Charles XVI fireplaces and *pietra serena* – but with flashes of eccentricity, such as the art deco zebra-skin ottomans and changing contemporary art in the lobby (left). Arch-renovator Michele Bönan's breakfast room is pure English country house, his candlelit roof terrace resembles a luxury yacht, and the basement lounge drips *A Clockwork Orange*'s Korova Milk Bar. Manager Claudio Meli has created an 'our house is your house' feel: guests can pour their own drinks and avail themselves of bespoke tours of the city. Book the penthouse to gaze on the Duomo (see p010) from your bathtub.
Piazza Santa Maria Novella 7,
T 055 264 5181, jkplace.com

Villa San Michele

Situated 8km north of town in the Fiesole hills, this impeccable hotel is the place to take a break from sightseeing. The former 15th-century Franciscan monastery has offered the full romantic package since 1952: stunning views from Henry White Cannon's stepped gardens, a pool, 46 luxe rooms and a shuttle to whizz you into town in 20 minutes. A restoration began in 1994, with interior designers JM Lay and Federico Forquet, and Pisa-based interiors company Puri pushing into every corner: the cloister is now the dining room, while the *limonaia* houses the Presidential Suite (above), which has a private terrace. We also like the spacious Michelangelo Suite. The façade of the building is thought to be the work of Michelangelo himself.
Via Doccia 4, Fiesole, T 055 567 8200, villasanmichele.com

24 HOURS

SEE THE BEST OF THE CITY IN JUST ONE DAY

Anyone attempting to bag Botticelli's *Birth of Venus* (Uffizi) and Michelangelo's *David* (Accademia) in one day should think again. Tsunamis of tourists attempt it every year, often throwing in the Medici Chapels (Piazza Madonna degli Aldobrandini 6, T 055 238 8602) for good measure, only to be defeated by gargantuan queues. You can beat the crowds by booking ahead (T 055 294 883), but the real trick is to seek out sublime works at lesser-known venues.

The Museo del Bargello (overleaf) offers masterworks aplenty without the crush, while Andrea del Sarto's Cenacolo (Via Andrea del Sarto 16, T 055 238 8603), a short walk east, is arguably the city's finest *Last Supper* fresco. South of the river is the relatively crowd-free Brancacci Chapel (Piazza del Carmine, T 055 238 2195), with works by Masolino and Masaccio. Far less taxing is the Salvatore Ferragamo Museum (Piazza Santa Trinita 5r, T 055 336 0456), home to some 13,000 pairs of shoes, the intoxicating scents of Officina Profumo Farmaceutica di Santa Maria Novella (see p086) and the contemporary photography at FOR Gallery (see p036).

Of course, such a demanding day should also include plenty of pitstops. Head to Caffè Concerto Paszkowski (opposite) for excellent breakfast brioches, stop for a midday reviver of home-made pasta at Olio & Convivium (see p081) and, to close the day, try Fabio Picchi's Teatro del Sale Alimentari (see p038).
For full addresses, see Resources.

09.00 Caffè Concerto Paszkowski

Leave the herds to Giubbe Rosse, Piazza della Repubblica's other big café, and kick off the day at the locals' choice. Owned by the Valenza family, with the affable Enrico Bolognini front of house, this 19th-century institution was once a favourite of Italy's literati, including D'Annunzio and Pratolini. Today, its wood-panelled walls and marble bar attract an egalitarian cross-section of Florentines – young professionals and families all jostle for some of the best *cappuccini* and brioche in town. The café prides itself on its delicate foodstuffs: the *pasticceria* lies on the lower-ground floor, so everything from the *cantucci* to the *soggetti di marzapane* is seconds from chef's touch. Look out for the dining room's trompe-l'œil portico (above). *Piazza della Repubblica 6r, T 055 210 236, paszkowski.it*

11.00 Museo del Bargello
The city's best sculpture collection
is oddly overlooked, letting you view
works, including Michelangelo's *Bacchus*,
in peace. The weaponry exhibits are
a macabre reminder that this palazzo
was once a prison where convicts
were hanged from the windows. It
re-opened as a museum in 1886.
*Via del Proconsolo 4, T 055 238 8606,
firenzemusei.it*

14.30 FOR Gallery
This 2008 photography gallery is a
hotbed of both established and new
talent. Founders Ori Kafri (owner of JK
Place, see p028), Fabrizio Moretti and
Riccardo Bacarelli (prime movers in
the art world) dig deep in their contacts
book to secure names such as Massimo
Listri and Giacomo Salizzoni (pictured).
*Via dei Fossi 45r, T 055 094 6444,
forgallery.it*

19.30 Teatro del Sale Alimentari

Picture a mix of rustic banquet, live show and religious sacrament, with a wild-eyed chef as MC, and you get some sense of what's in store here. Having joined for a few euros (there are 73,000 members worldwide) and bought your ticket for dinner, around £28, you plump for a seat at a communal table that instantly plunges you into wedding-style sociability. With a bellow loud enough to rattle the cutlery, chef Fabio Picchi then announces his first dish and steaming plates start flying from the kitchen onto a self-service table. Numerous servings of scrumptious risotto, polenta and macaroni later, and with each holler prompting a rush of diners, the night's theatricals begin. Shows run from madcap comedy courtesy of Picchi's wife, actress Maria Cassi, to more conventional jazz and classical concerts.
Via de' Macci 111r, T 055 200 1492, teatrodelsale.com

URBAN LIFE

CAFÉS, RESTAURANTS, BARS AND NIGHTCLUBS

Two decades ago, Florentines, accustomed to screeching up to the door of their favourite eaterie, suddenly found cars and Vespas banned from the *centro storico*. The result: petrol-friendly Oltrarno hangouts, such as breezy café AS Aurora (Viale Vasco Pratolini 2, T 055 224 059), now pull in the locals, leaving tourists to rule the central roosts. For proof, head for the 'city beach' strip on the south bank of the river between Ponte San Niccolò and Ponte alle Grazie. On summer weekends, gorgeous young *Fiorentini* absorb gallons of beer and pumping techno before flooding the riverbank for one almighty free-for-all. Head a little further west to witness the classic evening package – *apertivo* from 7pm, dinner at 9ish. The *nuovo-rustico* Il Santo Bevitore (Via Santo Spirito 66r, T 055 211 264) or Sant'Agostino 23 (Via Sant'Agostino 23r, T 055 210 208) are good bets, followed by bars like Dolce Vita (see p056).

For those keen to stay in the north, Rita Augier's Angels (Via del Proconsolo 29/31, T 055 239 8762) is one of the hipper central addresses, while musos head to Jazz Club Firenze (Via Nuova de' Caccini 3, T 055 247 9700) or Rex Café (Via Fiesolana, 25r, T 055 248 0331). And while the three-Michelin-starred Enoteca Pinchiorri (Via Ghibellina 87, T 055 242 777) offers some of the country's best fine dining, the budget-conscious should try the reasonably priced Ristorante del Fagioli (Corso Tintori 47r, T 055 244 285).

For all addresses, see Resources.

Quanto Basta

Alessandra Marino did a superb job with Rome's 'Gusto, and she's pulled out all the stops again for this multispace bar and restaurant, paces from the Duomo (see p010). Owned by sisters Alessandra and Elisa Ruggi, the feel is swanky butcher's shop meets trendy eaterie, the clinical white wall tiles broken by pendant lamps and benches. Here, Marino's trademark free-flowing scheme features a ground floor restaurant, an open kitchen and *salsamenteria* – a deli counter selling cold cuts of meat and slices of *taleggio* and *caprino* – and an enoteca perched on top of the spiral staircase showcasing nascent local estates. The food is rustic Tuscan, with an emphasis on organic produce, and features the likes of rabbit with olive caviar. *Via dei Ginori 10r, T 055 211 427, quantobasta.eu*

Golden View Open Bar
Set next to Ponte Vecchio, this buzzy
Tuscan diner is admittedly a tourist
magnet, but Tommaso Grasso should
be applauded for filling a gap in the
local restaurant scene. Marta Sansoni's
white interiors are light years from the
reworked innards of most palazzi and
the noon-1am opening hours are handy.
Via de' Bardi 58r, T 055 214 502,
www.goldenviewopenbar.com

Il Canapone

With room for just 26 diners, this boxy dining 'club' can hardly be a goldmine. But a few minutes spent with proprietors Valentina Mugnaini, Simone Riani and Antonella Mauro – and a glance at its palatable prices – and you realise that the destination is *la dolce vita* rather than *grossi profitti*. The current owners took over in 2004, redecorating Il Canapone every year, its 2008 incarnation a brash daubing of vermilion, green and yellow. The tone quietens with the trestle tables and cool white chairs – neutral backdrops for chef Riani's Japanese-tinged cuisine. Try the excellent tortellini in *brodo* (meat broth) and pistachio and honey ice cream. The pasta and ice cream are both made on the premises. The restaurant also hosts exhibitions and cookery courses.
Via Mazzetta 5a, T 055 238 1729

La Bussola
Founded in 1960 and once a late-night celeb haunt (catch the portraits of Steve Martin, John Grisham and Eros Ramazzoti behind the bar), Stefano Cresci's venue now caters for a middle-market tourist crowd. It remains, however, our top choice for the best solo perches in town: diners can bag a high chrome chair, rest their elbows on the Carrara marble counter and avoid solo-traveller syndrome with aplomb.

The menu bristles with Tuscan classics like porcini pasta, beef carpaccio and *bistecca alla fiorentina*, and there's a good choice of vin santo, grappa, artisanal beers and even a water list. And if the solitude still gets to you, head over the road to Slowly (T 055 264 5354) to lose yourself in the heaving-with-kids throng. *Via Porta Rossa 58r, T 055 293 376, labussolaflorence.com*

Cibrèo
Founded in 1979, the oldest of Fabio Picchi's eateries serves creative fare made with soul. As there's no menu, manager Cristina Petrelli takes you through the day's dishes. The wine list shows equal muster. Top choices include the Ferrari Perle' 2002, followed by the Morellino di Scansano Bronzone 2004.
Via Andrea del Verrocchio 8r,
T 055 234 1100, cibreo.com

Dolci & Dolcezza

East of the centre, Ilaria Balatresi's tiny *pasticceria* is a tour de force in fancy cakes. Try the classily packaged goods, such as the raspberry marmalade and chocolate tortes, and you'll see why this venue is treasured by locals. A pitstop also offers an insight into Florence's town planning. Look out of the window and you'll see the Porta alla Croce, a 13th-century gate in the (long gone) city wall, adorned with Michele di Ridolfo's fresco, *Madonna and Child and the Saints*. Giuseppe Poggi knocked the wall down in 1865 to make way for a ring road, more suited to the city's go-ahead status. *Piazza Cesare Beccaria 8r, T 055 234 5458*

Buca Lapi

'Thank you for putting the *dolce* back into the *vita*,' reads a scribble on a lampshade at Luciano Ghinassi's subterranean eaterie, located just off Via dei Tornabuoni. There's been a restaurant on this site since 1880, and while the waiters don't quite muster the moody charm of Marcello Mastroianni, the place looks every inch a scene from a Fellini classic. The tablecloths are pristine white, the walls are plastered with retro posters (Alitalia's Senegal and Morocco prints are among the best) and the kitchen turns out one of the tastiest *bistecca alla fiorentina* in town: a thud of Chianina T-bone, best accompanied by a bottle of Tignanello, an intense, chunky red from Tuscany's Antinori stable. Buca Lapi is open for dinner only.
Via del Trebbio 1r, T 055 213 768, bucalapi.com

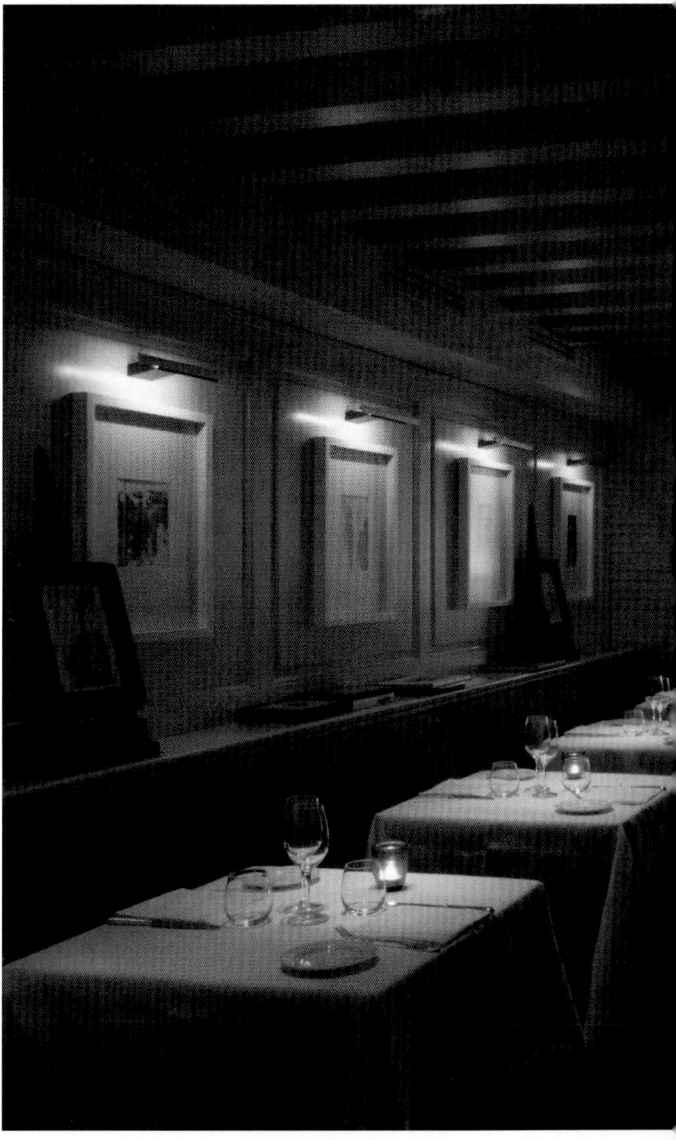

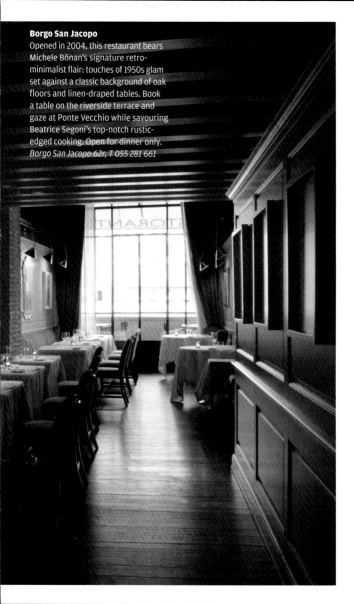

Borgo San Jacopo
Opened in 2004, this restaurant bears
Michele Bönan's signature retro-
minimalist flair: touches of 1950s glam
set against a classic background of oak
floors and linen-draped tables. Book
a table on the riverside terrace and
gaze at Ponte Vecchio while savouring
Beatrice Segoni's top-notch rustic-
edged cooking. Open for dinner only.
Borgo San Jacopo 62r, T 055 281 661

Boccanegra

Authentic *centro storico* restaurants are rarer than hen's teeth in this town, so Andrea Angelini's triple-eaterie is a godsend. Set on a corner opposite the Teatro Verde, the fine diner and *osteria* opened in 2000, while an adjoining ecclesiastical garment shop made way for a pizzeria in 2006. Spend a leisurely evening in the vaults of the atmospheric *osteria*, in the company of a Super Tuscan such as Ornellaia Masseto. Order chefs Alessandro Conffioni and Patrizio Vezzosi's mean *arista alla Toscana* (roast loin of pork) and *galletto marinato al mattone* (grilled marinated cockerel). If time is tight, opt for a tasty *caprese* in the pizzeria, along with in-the-know locals and pleasantly surprised tourists.
*Via Ghibellina 124r, Via Verdi 27r,
T 055 200 1098, boccanegra.com*

Garbo

Having cracked 'refined rustic' with their Oltrarno eaterie Filipepe (T 055 200 1397), Francesco Corniglio and Gianni Giorgi plumped for polar purity with Garbo, which opened in 2008. Designer Corina Peppino created an interior of clinical white, softened by elements such as abstract artworks. The gallery look is intentional – Garbo puts on regular exhibitions. The kitchen produces the ballast to stop the place floating off in puffy conceptual clouds. Order a classic Tuscan dish such as duck breast with rosemary, sip some Quattro Chiacchere chardonnay and ponder.
Borgo San Frediano 25, T 055 295 311, garbo-borgosanfrediano.com

Oibò

With beefy security and press agents on hand at the click of a Prada heel, Matteo Peruzzi's bar is one of Florence's hotspots. Tourists cram its pavement tables to goggle at Piazza Santa Croce's basilica (see p065), while the interior is tailor-made for parties. Andrè Benaim has done a nice job on the interiors: the orange bar bears a foliage motif, and a striking purple and pink sea anemone of a chandelier dominates the upstairs. In the kitchen, Simone Gronchi, Alessio Angione and Tommaso Fiorenzani put new twists on traditional fare, creating the likes of beef carpaccio with porcini. *Via dei Benci 53r, T 055 263 8611, oibo.net*

Cavalli Club

This Oltrarno nightclub, the first from Roberto Cavalli, is a perfect encapsulation of the Florentine fashion designer's ostentatious style. Crafted out of a former 15th-century church, the interiors – a riot of fluorescent lighting, metallic surfaces and animal print – were conceived by the Milan-based Studio Italo Rota & Partners. The ground floor houses the bar and a stage for DJ sets, and an upper level was created to accommodate a slightly more serene restaurant, serving Tuscan cuisine on Cavalli-designed tableware. Expect jazz and lounge sounds, stylish-looking cocktails and lots of models.
Piazza del Carmine 8r, T 055 211 650, robertocavalli.com

Dolce Vita
Boasting that essential Italian bar
accessory, a massive car park out front,
this is Oltrarno's post-dinner honeyspot,
swarming with lively *Fiorentini* until 2am.
Founded in 1985, its secret lies in regular
makeovers: Claudio Nardi, architect and
owner of Riva Lofts (see p021) has been
responsible for one interior, while a recent
look comes courtesy of Gaetano Pesce.
The New York-based architect and interior
designer created three distinctive spaces:
a candelabra-lit DJ lair with an orange
booth, a smooth curve of a main bar, and
an intimate room with banquette seating.
The cocktail list displays a nationalistic
streak and should keep you coming
back for more, but the real fun lies in
watching the people.
Piazza del Carmine, T 055 284 595,
dolcevitaflorence.com

Alle Murate

Renaissance portraiture has never been so palatable. This medieval palazzo, restored by Danelia Dini and Maria Monica Donato, is home to the earliest known likenesses of Dante and Boccaccio, in addition to archaeological remains dating to Roman times. A tour of these 14th-century frescoes can be followed by a meal at Umberto Montano's fine-dining restaurant, where chef Elio di Franco's menu is classic Italian. Alle Murate also gives you another opportunity to admire the beautiful restoration work. While the entrance and lower-ground floor have had a minimalist makeover with a tongue of clean-lined natural wood and discreet lighting, the vaults retain their frescoed glory. Open for dinner only.
Via del Proconsolo 16r, T 055 240 618, www.artenotai.com

Plasma

Davide Rizzo's latest urban offering is situated south of the Arno on the corner of Piazza Ferrucci. Drawing inspiration from bars in Shanghai, London and New York, Giancarlo Cauteruccio remade the bar's two floors in autumn 2008: 42in plasma screens, epoxy resin floors and fibre-optic lighting abound. There's even a waterfall for aqua-assisted screenings. The main bar – a fat red-resin curve – is located on the ground floor, and in the basement there's a cavernous gallery space, complete with glass bar. Although Plasma is open in the evenings only to the general public, Rizzo is targeting the corporate market too, with PowerPoint-friendly kit available for meetings, launches and press conferences. *Piazza Francesco Ferrucci 1r, T 055 051 6926, virtualplasma.it*

Yab

If it cuts the mustard for NYC promoter Fatman Scoop, this OTT club is good enough for the tripping weekender. Situated just east of Palazzo Strozzi, Yab, whose interiors were designed by Lorenzo Gemma, administers doses of house, garage and pseudo-gangsta hip hop to a loyal following of young Italians. Deckhand rosters mix top Italian DJs – Fabio KF, Mauro Ferrucci and Miky Garzilli have all donned headphones here – with international stars like Michael Canitrot from Paris and Delicious of Miami Beach fame. Prepare for a dancefloor prickling with coloured lights. Once you've proved your credentials out there, repair to the restaurant for energy-boosting pasta.
Via de' Sassetti 5r, T 055 215 160, yab.it

INSIDER'S GUIDE

ELENA MORETTI, JOURNALIST

Elena Moretti is a freelance writer for *Corriere della Sera*, *Firenze* magazine and Florence-based fashion company Pitti Immagine. She lives on the southern slopes of Fiesole. Moretti likes to kickstart her day with a perfect cappuccino ('a light dusting of cocoa is a must') at Caffè Giacosa (Via della Spada 10r, T 055 277 6328), located on the borders of Santa Maria Novella and San Giovanni. Originally opened in 1815, the café was renovated and relaunched by its new owner, Roberto Cavalli, in 2002.

For lunch, she heads to Oltrarno, to tuck into some of her favourite food – a plate of seafood – at the rustic Borgo Antico (Piazza Santo Spirito 6r, T 055 210 437). Then it's back over the river to San Marco, for a mid-afternoon hot-stone massage at Soulspace (see p089), 'the best place in town to recharge'.

Come *aperitivo* hour, she likes Zoe' (Via dei Renai 13r, T 055 243 111). In summer, the terrace at Nove (Piazza degli Scarlatti 1r, T 055 230 2756) is a place to see and be seen, while in winter, Moretti takes a table at Prince Dimitri Kunz d'Asburgo Lorena's La Giostra (Borgo Pinti 12r, T 055 241 341). 'The *spianata di chianina* (beef sandwich) is a great order.' Colle Bereto (Piazza Strozzi 5r, T 055 283 156) is where she sips an after-dinner Attico or two ('they still won't tell me the ingredients'), before heading to Rooms Club (Via della Fornace 9, T 333 591 0461) for its music and art projections. *For full addresses, see Resources.*

ARCHITOUR

A GUIDE TO FLORENCE'S ICONIC BUILDINGS

If it's new and more than four inches high, stand by for fireworks. From Arata Isozaki's proposed Uffizi loggia, which was scrapped in 2005, to the city's tram system, meddling government officials and archaeological finds have stymied even the most inspired new build. Remarkably, some modern(ish) structures did make it through the planning mill, many propelled by Mussolini's clunking fist: Michelucci's boxy Stazione Santa Maria Novella (Piazza della Stazione, T 055 235 6120); Angiolo Mazzoni's now rather forlorn 1934 Complesso Centrale Termica SMN (Via delle Ghiacciaie), complete with periscope frontispiece; and Pierluigi Nervi's 1931 Stadio Artemio Franchi (see p090). For more recent edifices, you'll have to pedal out of town. Banished to the suburbs are Leonardo Savioli and Leonardo Ricci's sprawling housing project, Case Popolari di Sorgane (Viale Benedetto Croce), built between 1963 and 1980, Lando Bartoli's Sacro Cuore (see p013) and Giovanni Michelucci's sublime Chiesa di San Giovanni Battista (see p069).

There is hope for the future, though. Leonardo Ricci's long-awaited Nuovo Palazzo di Giustizia (see p014) has finally taken shape. Work is well underway on the tram system, and Foster + Partners' epic railway station, slated for completion in 2010, with its platforms 25m below ground, proved too critical a part of Italy's new rail network to be severed by the planners' scalpel.

For full addresses, see Resources.

Basilica di Santa Croce

Architecture by Arnolfo di Cambio, frescoes and stained glass by Giotto, Michelangelo's tomb, Donatello's *Annunciation* – this Franciscan church complex, completed in 1294, has all the hits but none of the Duomo frenzy. A tour around Vasari's interior and tombs of the city's luminaries, including Niccolò Machiavelli, can be followed by a quiet wander around the cloister gardens, home to Henry Moore's

Warrior and temporary sculpture exhibits. The plain 1470 Pazzi Chapel, designed by Brunelleschi, is a must-visit, shards of sunlight piercing the dome, as is the museum, where you can see Gaddi's *Last Supper* and Orcagna's fragmented fresco. *Piazza Santa Croce, T 055 244 619, santacroce.firenze.it*

Casa per Appartamenti
One of the city's most heart-warming structures, Leonardo Savioli and Danilo Santi's concrete flats, finished in 1967, were clearly influenced by the metabolist movement's modular housing. The apartments have a slightly madcap air, comprising interlocking blocks of grey concrete and weathered wooden shutters, topped by an ellipsoidal roof.
Via Piagentina 79

Pensilina Stazione SMN

Even a humble bus terminal has to punch above its weight in this town. Opened in 1990, and designed by architects Cristiano Toraldo di Francia and Andrea Noferi, this slice of marble looks more like a stubby-nosed prototype submarine, complete with porthole windows, than a municipal transport hub. Its aluminium roof, however, does provide some pretty stylish shelter for the millions of tourists who visit the city. Inevitably, the radical design prompted a flurry of ire from some quarters. Architecture critic Gianni Pettena branded the composition 'imprudent' and the product of a 'youthful attempt to combine numerous erudite references'.
Via Valfonda

Chiesa di San Giovanni Battista

Life-affirming, biomorphic and plain weird – if only most churches could look like this. Hugging the A1 Naples-Milan autostrada, 25-minutes' drive north-west of the city, Giovanni Michelucci's creation was built between 1961 and 1964 in memory of workers who died in the construction of the motorway network. It's a million miles from Michelucci's Fascist commissions, such as the railway station (see p064), comprising a jostle of parabolas encased in pink-and-white stone, punctured with strips of glass and crowned by a billowing roof of concrete and copper. Visitors pass through Pericle Fazzini's intimidating bronze doors to enter an interior dotted with statues. Open Monday to Saturday, 9am-4.30pm.
Campi Bisenzio, A1 Uscita Firenze Nord, T 055 421 9016

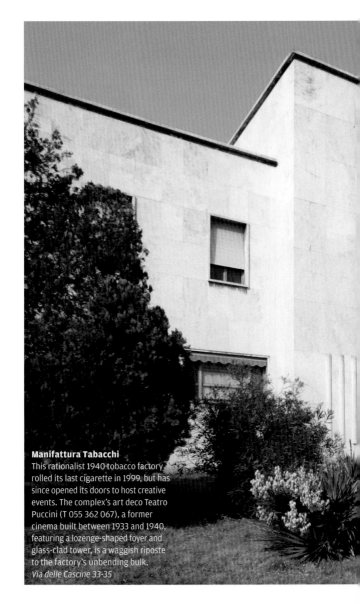

Manifattura Tabacchi
This rationalist 1940 tobacco factory rolled its last cigarette in 1999, but has since opened its doors to host creative events. The complex's art deco Teatro Puccini (T 055 362 067), a former cinema built between 1933 and 1940, featuring a lozenge-shaped foyer and glass-clad tower, is a waggish riposte to the factory's unbending bulk.
Via delle Cascine 33-35

SHOPPING
THE BEST RETAIL THERAPY AND WHAT TO BUY

Florence is the product of centuries of artisan graft, with its silk, wool and leather trades creating powerful guilds of merchants and bankers in the 13th century. Zip forward to the 20th century, and Tuscan-born brands Gucci and Salvatore Ferragamo conquered the fashion world. Today, both satisfy shoppers' pangs, the backstreet workshops still thriving across the river from the super-labels.

For your hit of the big players, head to San Giovanni. Via dei Tornabuoni and the streets around Piazza della Repubblica are a seemingly endless catwalk, including the stores of Fendi, Louis Vuitton, Gucci and Dolce & Gabbana. If you're looking for a one-stop shop, call into Luisa Via Roma (overleaf), a long-established fashion emporium selling Roberta di Camerino, Mauro Vanzi and Gastone Lucioli, among many others. Lungarno Details (Lungarno Acciaiuoli 4, T 055 2726 8000) is Ferragamo's interiors showcase. For vintage furniture, go east to Tre di Denari (see p084), calling ahead first to make sure the shop is open. Perfume aficionados should make for Olfattorio (opposite) and the unmatched Officina Profumo Farmaceutica di Santa Maria Novella (see p086).

South of the river, the districts of San Frediano and Santo Spirito are the city's artisanal heartlands. Martino Titto offers an up-to-date take on the area's heritage at Giofrè (Via Sant' Agostino 30/32r, T 055 239 9141), where the streetwear is made in front of you. *For full addresses, see Resources.*

Olfattorio

Spraying a fragrant plume into Florence's premier shopping street is this minimalist perfumery, opened by Giovanni Gaidano and Renata De Rossi in 2007. To step over the threshold is to walk into a giant lava coolbox; the walls and central display counter radiate fractured volcanic orange. There are more than 200 varieties of scent on sale, but the real attraction lies in the emporium's tiny museum. Here

you'll find a fine collection of antique perfume bottles; gems include Bertelli's 1925 art nouveau Vellutina Venus and the French 1930 Gemey perfume bottle that has a delicate speckled hen's egg patina. *Via dei Tornabuoni 6, T 055 286 925, www.olfattorio.it*

Luisa Via Roma
Its plasma screens and concrete-and-glass interiors belie the fact that this three-level shop dates back to the 1930s. Reimagined in 2008 by local design studio Claudio Nardi Architects, Florence's best known *alta moda* boutique sells a well-edited selection of mens- and womenswear. International designers rub shoulders with Florentine labels Nanà, Lucioli and Mauro Vanzi, and there are limited-edition pieces from the likes of Lanvin, DSquared and Givenchy. The service is equally high-spec. Touch-screen computers allow shoppers to select the garments they would like to see waiting for them in their dressing room, and there's a suite above the store available for private shopping, complete with a bedroom, bathroom and kitchen with chef on hand.
Via Roma 19-21r, T 055 906 4116,
luisaviaroma.com

'Ino

Alessandro Frassica made the obvious career choice with his deli, a neat space tucked away a few paces north of the Arno. As an occasional food writer, he spent much of his time scouring Italy for small producers of rarefied comestibles. His travails have paid off: his shop is full of below-the-radar goodies, such as Chianina ragú, honey from Castagno, and gorgonzola swimming with anchovies.

There's a small section – essentially a clutch of rustic barrels with glass tops and wooden counters – where shoppers can sample the goods before purchasing, and an inviting counter of cheese, salami and pasta, plus some tasty takeaway *panini*. Frassica still offers journalistic musings on his witty blog.
Via dei Georgofili 3r/7r, T 055 219 208, ino-firenze.com

Catalpa

The catalpa tree bears beautiful orchid-like flowers, and its leafy shade attracts an eclectic cross-section of birdlife. A suitable moniker then for Luca Berti's shop, which is part sartorial showcase, part lifestyle store. Opened in September 2008, it offers Berti's own womenswear, alongside jewellery, goat's-milk-based toiletries from Chianti, coffee cups, vases and perfume. Look out too for clothes by Alberta Ferretti, Sonia Rykiel and Neil Barrett. If you ever find yourself in Ferrara, visit Berti's other store (T 051 683 2406). *Via della Spada 36r, Via del Sole 15r, T 055 216 997, catalpa.it*

Domus Aurea
Paolo Tozzi spends much of the year
travelling around the world in search of
furniture and objets d'art, picking up
items such as chandeliers, 18th-century
tables, ornate nightingale cages and
gym horses. Fortunately, Tozzi's eye for
rarities and oddball items puts his
collection well beyond the realm of faddish
retro kitsch. His emporium, opened in
1999 and tucked away in Oltrarno a few
yards south of Ponte alla Carraia, proffers
classics from the moment you cross the
threshold, so be prepared for 19th-
century French blue-stone tables with
fleur-de-lys detailing at every turn, or
a film set's worth of vintage lamps and
lighting rigs. And if an ornate stone bench
won't quite fit in your bag, you could
always hop back home with a pair of 19th-
century frogs made from Calcarea stone.
Via dei Serragli 9r, T 055 291 699

Pineider

If your calfskin letter opener has finally given up the ghost, this central emporium could come to the rescue. Francesco Pineider founded his stationery business on this site in 1774; today, it's a sleek, two-storey flagship of a global brand that stretches from San Francisco to Seoul. The collection includes handmade *veau grainé* briefcases, bowling bags, calfskin and mahogany humidors and pens.

The brand is staying true to its roots, with a good stock of watermarked paper and a printing service for personalised invitations, greeting cards and even wine labels. Also check out the leather wares of Paolo Carandini (T 055 245 397). *Piazza della Signoria 13/14r, T 055 284 655, pineider.com*

Olio & Convivium

Founded in 1980 with the aim of preserving Tuscan and Florentine culinary traditions, Convivium Firenze is now a byword for upmarket delicacies. The brand has since expanded to catering, a cantina, cookery courses and an online shop, but its Oltrarno deli/restaurant, Olio & Convivium, which is managed by Tommaso Vezzani and Massimo Maturi, and designed by Riccardo Barthel, is the pièce de résistance. Built into Palazzo Capponi, it sells artfully presented foods including pasta sauces, honey, and biscuits from the Convivium brand, launched in 2006. A restaurant serves the likes of *straccetti di maiale* (pork fillet steak), and homemade ravioli. There's a sister deli/eaterie in the southeast of town (T 055 680 2482).
Via Santo Spirito 4, T 055 265 8198,
www.conviviumfirenze.it

46 Santo Spirito
Jacopo Bruscoli's store was designed
by MRM Architetti Associati, who filled
this vaulted south-of-the-river space
with distinctive oil-black cabinets.
Founded in 2007, it sells men's and
women's shoes and clothes by Italian
designers, art and wine – on Friday
nights, the venue morphs into a bar.
*Via Santo Spirito 46r, T 055 210 659,
46santospirito.com*

Tre di Denari

This store has all the architectural finesse of a rickety conservatory, but the wares are undisputed design classics. Vera Beck has scoured the length and breadth of Italy to track down 1950s, 60s and 70s lamps, tables and other assorted retro items. As a result, her shop, tucked away on the north flank of Piazza Sant'Ambrogio, is rammed with wonders by the likes of Franco Albini, Ettore Sottsass, Guzzini and Tobia Scarpe. South-east of Tre di Denari is Sant'Ambrogio market, a more authentic alternative to the much vaunted Mercato di San Lorenzo. This mid-18th century pavilion is where you'll find locals doing their daily shop, picking up ravioli, cheese, figs, artichokes and tomatoes.
Piazza Sant'Ambrogio, T 055 200 1698

Farmaceutica di Santa Maria Novella
Founded in the 13th century by Dominican
friars, this pharmacy is one of kind. Amid
the scores of scents are Acqua della Regina,
created for Caterina De' Medici, Queen of
France in the 16th century. The sales room
is breathtaking; a red carpet swooshes
up to a high altar of a sales counter. Don't
miss the ornate chapel and garden.
Via della Scala 16, T 055 216 276,
www.smnovella.it

SPORTS AND SPAS
WORK OUT, CHILL OUT OR JUST WATCH

This being an Italian city, staying in shape was always going to be more about buff and preen than elliptical cross trainers and dank subterranean gyms. The pools and saunas at Klab (Via de Conti 7, T 055 213 514) and Tropos (Via Orcagna, 20a, T 055 678 381) offer ample opportunity to show off your tone, but the outdoor pool Le Pavoniere in Parco delle Cascine (Via della Catena 2, T 055 333 979), open between May and September, cuts to the chase; it's an excuse for en masse posing to a DJ soundtrack.

This obsession with beauty has infiltrated the artisan heartlands south of the river. Wave (Via Santo Spirito 27, T 055 265 4650) is a retro-glam beauty clinic, while nearby is Dr Georgios Foukis's shiny medical aesthetics centre, Skin Aesthetic Clinic (see p092), staffed by surgeons, dermatologists, dentists and nutritionists. Fortunately, rugged non-exhibitionists have options too: Jolita Trahan's studio Touch (Via Giuseppe Giusti 6r, T 055 248 0956) offers Pilates, while tough nuts can join Mauro Taiuti (T 335 802 4833) for a horse trek through the Tuscan countryside or pull on snowshoes to climb the 1,654m Mt Falterona. And to prove that Florentine men aren't all chest waxes and pedicures, select hardmen congregate on Piazza Santa Croce every June to slug it out in *calcio storico* matches. Dating to the 15th century, these rugby-style tussles involve few rules and plenty of bare-knuckle fighting. *For full addresses, see Resources.*

Soulspace

Zelal Elbistan's spa and beauty centre is a nerve-soothing bolthole created by architects Stefano Mannucci and Lorenzo Leoncini, just a few paces east of the Duomo (see p010). Launched in 2007, it's rated as one of the city's top spas, with treatments running from conventional massages to anti-ageing cell-regeneration facials and exotic scrubs. The day packages are a good option, offering combos of pool, hammam, massage and reflexology sessions to suit your mood. The real boon, though, is the interior, from the low-lit putty-grey reception to the shimmering jade pool and the marble-clad hammam. And if you fear you'll never surface from your reverie, try a few sharp intakes of air in the pretty decked garden.
Via Sant'Egidio 12, T 055 200 1794, soulspace.it

Stadio Artemio Franchi

ACF Fiorentina's home ground sprouted in 1931, bearing all the bombastic symmetry and quake-in-your-boots scale of classic Mussolini-era builds. Designed by Pierluigi Nervi and Alessandro Giuntoli, it's a graceful symphony in reinforced concrete, supported by helix staircases and towering neoclassical columns, and topped by a strident 70m tower. Originally named after Fascist vigilante Giovanni Berta, it now sports the more palatable moniker of Artemio Franchi after the late Italian Football Federation president. The 47,000-plus seater was spruced up for the 1990 FIFA World Cup, and sits among the city's key sporting venues, which include the Stadio Luigi Ridolfi, used for athletics (T 055 262 5169).
Viale Manfredo Fanti 4, T 055 503 011, it.violachannel.tv/artemio-franchi

Skin Aesthetic Clinic
Plastic surgeon Dr Georgios Foukis hired
architect Michael Young to design his clinic
after seeing his work in Wallpaper*.
On the ground floor of the 12th-century
Torre dei Barbadori, Young and Icelandic
artist Katrin Olina created a serene space
with floral Corian floors, backlit walls and
pod-like treatment rooms. The consulting
room looks onto the Ponte Vecchio.
Borgo San Jacopo 64r, T 055 274 1503

Atletica Firenze Marathon
Originally built for the Italian military,
this fitness centre is now under the
muscular management of sports agencies
Firenze Marathon and Atletica Firenze
Marathon. Designed by Roman engineer
Dario Bugli, it offers personal trainers,
tennis, five-a-side football, a gym and
a good range of classes.
Viale Malta 10, T 055 679 693,
www.firenzeatletica.it

ESCAPES

WHERE TO GO IF YOU WANT TO LEAVE TOWN

Tuscany's rolling hills have the power to revive the most frazzled visitor, even if it's just a quick ice cream and a stroll in Fiesole. Further afield, phalanxes of coach arrivals have put hill towns such as San Gimignano under siege. Lesser-known destinations like Volterra, 80km south of Florence, have Etruscan fortifications and Renaissance palaces and are relatively untrammelled.

The secret of enjoying the area, however, lies in holing up in a small-scale retreat. Montepulciano's Bioagriturismo Fattoria San Martino (Via Martiena 3, T 057 871 7463) is pushing the organic envelope – the villa has been restored using eco materials and there's a chemical-free bio-pond for dips – while the 4,500-acre Castiglion del Bosco private membership estate (T 057 780 7078) offers exclusive stays within the Val d'Orcia park. Wine lovers should head for Fattoria di Rignana (Via di Rignana 15, T 055 852 065) in Chianti, which is surrounded by 120 hectares of vineyards and olive groves. Cosimo Gericke and Sveva Rocco di Torrepadula have renovated the 17th-century villa to accommodate 16 people, and offer tours and tastings. Time-pressed oenophiles should settle for lunch at Osteria di Passignano (Via Passignano 33, T 055 807 1278) in the Vallombrosa Abbey. And if you haven't had your fill of Medici *braggadocio*, visit one of their villas, Villa Medicea La Petraia (Via di Castello, T 055 451 208), which boasts a garden by Tribolo. *For full addresses, see Resources.*

Rocca di Frassinello, Giuncarico

Spain's winery scene has its showboaters, notably Frank Gehry's Marqués de Riscal in the Rioja region, but Renzo Piano and Mario Botta are keeping the Tuscan end up with characteristic Italian brio. Opened in 2007, Rocca di Frassinello is Piano's first winery. Located 165km south-west of Florence, near the coastal town Castiglione della Pescaia, you'll have no trouble finding it. Constructed of steel and terracotta-coloured cement, its tower looms large on the horizon. Inside, the 40m tiered cellar (overleaf) resembles an amphitheatre and holds 2,500 *barriques* containing the fruits of a venture between the Italian Castellare and French Rothschild estates. Botta's Petra Suvereto (T 056 584 5308) is 145km south-west of Florence in San Lorenzo Alto. *Comune di Gavorrano, T 056 688 400, castellare.it*

Cellar, Rocca di Frassinello

Pietrasanta
This 'City of Artists' situated 10km north of Viareggio was founded in the 13th century and is packed with studios, workshops and sculptures hewn from nearby marble quarries. Michelangelo and Miró carved here while Fernando Botero is today's big sculptor. Head to the Museo dei Bozzetti (pictured). *Via Sant' Agostino 1, T 058 479 5500, www.museodeibozzetti.com*

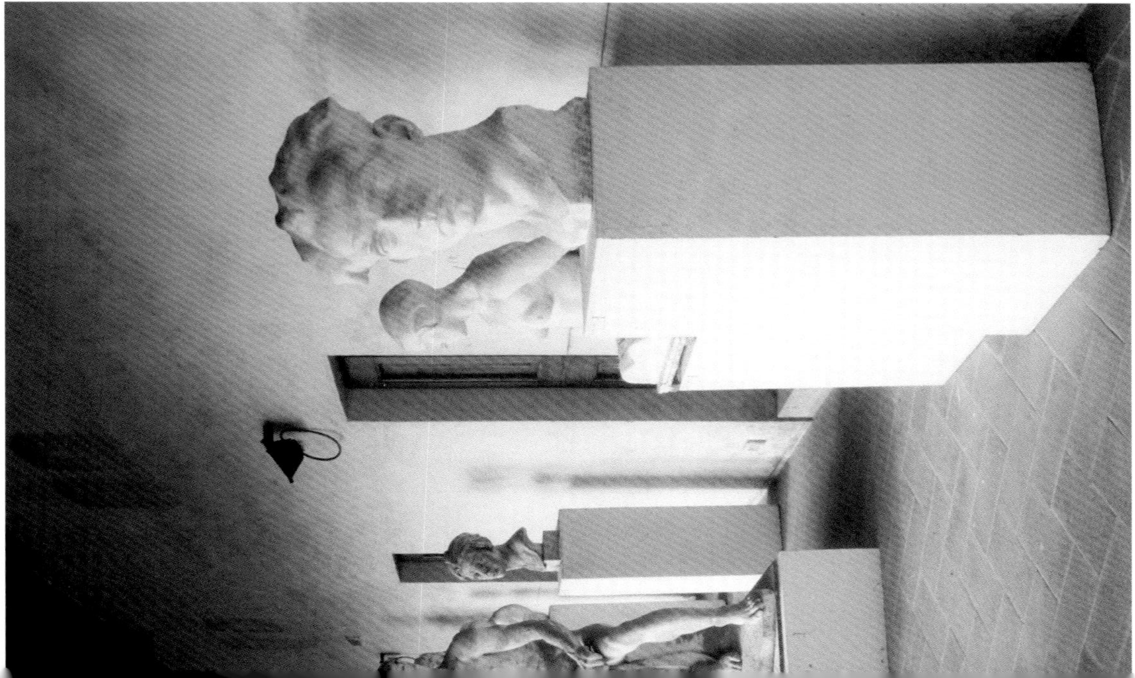

Palazzo Orlandi, Prato

Sabrina Bignami's guesthouse in Italy's textile capital, Prato, is a tour de force in restoration and modern design. The architect, whose projects include a Florentine factory renovation and a sushi bar in Nagoya, discovered the crumbling 18th-century palazzo in 2004. The original floors and windows were intact, while under layers of paint lay Luigi Catani's frescoes of pastoral scenes and fluttering *putti*. Bignami has pulled off a gorgeous three-room guesthouse (Pink Room, above), installing modernist pieces, such as Saarinen furniture, and Corian-bedecked bathrooms in a period setting. In town, do visit the Centro per l'Arte Contemporaneo Luigi Pecci (T 057 453 17), designed by Italo Gamberini and showing pieces by Anish Kapoor and Mauro Staccioli.
Via Giozzelmi 9, T 335 526 0860, b-arch.it

NOTES
SKETCHES AND MEMOS

RESOURCES

CITY GUIDE DIRECTORY

HOTELS

ADDRESSES AND ROOM RATES

Bioagriturismo Fattoria
San Martino 096
Room rates:
double, €120
Via Martiena 3
Montepulciano
T 057 871 7463
fattoriasanmartino.it
Castiglion del Bosco 096
Room rates:
suites, from €600
Località Castiglion del Bosco
Montalcino
T 057 780 7078
www.castigliondelbosco.it
Continentale Contemporary
Pleasing Hotel 016
Room rates:
double, from €200
Vicolo dell'Oro 6r
T 055 27 262
lungarnohotels.com
Fattoria di Rignana 096
Room rates:
double, €105
Via di Rignana 15
Chianti
T 055 852 065
rignana.it
Four Seasons Hotel 017
Room rates:
double, €325;
Room 122, €2,200;
Della Gherardesca Royal Suite, €15,950
Borgo Pinti 99
T 055 26 261
fourseasons.com/florence

Gallery Hotel Art 020
Room rates:
double, €330;
Penthouse San Miniato, €890
Vicolo dell'Oro 5
T 055 27 263
lungarnohotels.com
Helvetia & Bristol 016
Room rates:
double, from €539
Via dei Pescioni 2
T 055 26 651
royaldemeure.com
JK Place 028
Room rates:
double, €350;
Penthouse, €800
Piazza Santa Maria Novella 7
T 055 264 5181
jkplace.com
Hotel Lungarno 016
Room rates:
double, from €429
Borgo San Jacopo 14
T 055 27 261
lungarnohotels.com
Palazzo Orlandi 102
Room rates:
double, from €200;
Pink Room, from €200
Via Giozzelmi 9
Prato
T 335 526 0860
b-arch.it

Palazzo Tornabuoni 027
Room rates:
Studio Category membership, €239,800
Via dei Tornabuoni 16
T 055 268 966
palazzotornabuoni.com
Relais Santa Croce 026
Room rates:
double, €605;
Suite Dei Pepi, €1,900;
Suite Da Verrazzano, €3,025
Via Ghibellina 87
T 055 234 2230
relaissantacroce.com
Riva Lofts 021
Room rates:
double, €210;
Studio Seven, €240;
Loft studio, €550
Via Baccio Bandinelli 98
T 055 713 0272
rivahotel.it
Hotel Savoy 016
Room rates:
double, €561
Piazza della Repubblica 7
T 055 27 351
roccofortecollection.com
Stanze di Santa Croce 016
Room rates:
double, from €176
Via delle Pinzochere 6
T 347 259 3010
lestanzedisantacroce.com
Le Tre Stanze 016
Room rates:
double, from €120
Via dell'Oriuolo 43
T 329 2128 756
letrestanze.it

UNA Hotel Vittoria 024
Room rates:
double, Executive Room
and Superior Room, €486
Via Pisana 59
T 055 22 771
unahotels.it
Villa La Vedetta 022
Room rates:
double, from €189;
Bellavista Suite, from €699
Viale Michelangelo 78
T 055 681 631
www.villalavedettahotel.com
Villa San Michele 030
Room rates:
double, €945;
Presidential Suite, €3,740;
Michelangelo Suite, €2,695
Via Doccia 4
Fiesole
T 055 567 8200
villasanmichele.com
Westin Excelsior 016
Room rates:
double, from €870
Piazza Ognissanti 3
T 055 27 151
starwoodhotels.com

WALLPAPER* CITY GUIDES

Editorial Director
Richard Cook

Art Director
Loran Stosskopf
Editor
Rachael Moloney
Author
Jonathan Lee
Deputy Editor
Jeremy Case
Managing Editor
Jessica Diamond

Chief Designer
Daniel Shrimpton
Designer
Lara Collins

Map Illustrator
Russell Bell

Photography Editor
Sophie Corben
Photography Assistant
Robin Key

Sub-Editors
James Lamb
Alison Willmott
Editorial Assistant
Ella Marshall

Interns
Kim Fischer
Lucy Mapstone
Cat Tsang
Yvette Yarnold

**Wallpaper* Group
Editor-in-Chief**
Tony Chambers
Publishing Director
Gord Ray

Contributors
Roberta Berni
Lorenzo and Antonella
Gambacorta
Sara Henrichs
Elisabetta Paroli
Patrick-John Steiner
Emiliano Tagliaferri
Nick Vinson

Wallpaper* ® is a
registered trademark
of IPC Media Limited

All prices are correct at
time of going to press,
but are subject to change.

PHAIDON

Phaidon Press Limited
Regent's Wharf
All Saints Street
London N1 9PA

Phaidon Press Inc
180 Varick Street
New York, NY 10014

Phaidon® is a registered
trademark of Phaidon
Press Limited

www.phaidon.com

First published 2009
© 2009 IPC Media Limited

ISBN 978 0 7148 4910 2

A CIP Catalogue record for
this book is available from
the British Library.

All rights reserved.
No part of this publication
may be reproduced, stored
in a retrieval system or
transmitted, in any form
or by any means,
electronic, mechanical,
photocopying, recording
or otherwise, without
the prior permission of
Phaidon Press.

Printed in China

PHOTOGRAPHERS

Per Andersen/Alamy
Florence city view, inside
front cover

Michael Denance
Rocca di Frassinello, p097,
pp098-099

Nathalie Krugg
Casa Orlandi, Prato, p102

Massimo Listri
FOR Gallery, pp036-037

Nicolas Mathéus
Casa Orlandi, Prato, p103

**James McConnachie/
DK Images**
Stadio Artemio Franchi,
pp090-091

Oliviero Olivieri
Duomo, pp010-011
Palazzo Vecchio, p012
Sacro Cuore, p013
Nuovo Palazzo di Giustizia,
pp015-016
Four Seasons Hotel, p017
Gallery Hotel Art, p020
Riva Lofts, p021
Relais Santa Croce, p026
Villa San Michele,
p030, p031

Caffè Concerto
Paszkowski, p033
Museo del Bargello,
pp034-035
Teatro del Sale Alimentari,
pp038-039
Quanto Basta, p041
Golden VIew Open Bar,
pp042-043
Canapone, p044
La Bussola, p045
Cibrèo, pp046-047
Dolci & Dolcezza, 048
Buca Lapi, p049
Borgo San Jacopo,
pp050-051
Boccanegra, p052
Garbo, p053
Oibò, p054
Dolce Vita, pp056-057
Alle Murate, p058
Plasma, p059
Yab, pp060-061
Elena Moretti, p063
Basilica di Santa
Croce, p065
Casa per Appartamenti,
pp066-067
Chisea di San Giovanni
Battista, p069
Manifattura Tabacchi,
pp070-071
Olfattorio, p073
'Ino, p076
Catalpa, p077
Domus Aurea, pp078-079
Pineider, p080

Olio & Convivium, p081
46 Santo Spirito,
pp082-083
Tre di Denari, pp084-085
Officina Profumo
Farmaceutica di Santa
Maria Novella, pp086-087
Soulspace, p089
Wellness Firenze
Marathon, p094-095

Gianni Triolo
Four Seasons Hotel,
pp018-019

FLORENCE

A COLOUR-CODED GUIDE TO THE HOT 'HOODS

SANTA MARIA NOVELLA
Michelucci's station, San Lorenzo market and swish hotels counterpoint the churches

SAN MARCO
Ditch the crowds beelining for the Accademia with a tour of this area's elegant gardens

CAMPO DI MARTE
Catch an AFC Fiorentina game or view some of the city's best modern architecture

OLTRARNO
South of the Arno is where you'll find the happening bars and some great retail haunts

SANTA CROCE
Locals come here for the best food market in town and the area's top-notch restaurants

SAN GIOVANNI
It's all here – the major Renaissance sights, the super-brand shops and swarms of tourists

For a full description of each neighbourhood, see the Introduction.
Featured venues are colour-coded, according to the district in which they are located.